The Little Book of Learning Experience Design: A Beginner's Guide to Creating Great Learning Experiences for Today's Corporate Environments

By Kiersten Yocum, PhD

Chapters

1 - What is this book anyway?   5

2 - Formal Shmormal: The new way of learning   9

3 – What the heck is Learning Experience Design?   23

4 – What we adults like   31

5 – Who you talkin' to?   41

6 – Beg, buy or build   55

7 - It's all about the experience   75

8 – If you build it, they're not gonna come… unless you tell them about it   97

9 – Keep on keepin' on   109

Appendix A: Resources   117

1 - What is this book anyway?

This book is about designing learning experiences. That's why it's called The Little Book of Learning Experience Design, duh. But what is Learning Experience Design? You'll find out as you read more. For now, and for our purposes, know that Learning Experience Design is the newest form of instructional design.

Anyone can be an instructional designer. You are likely reading this book because you do some of that instructional design stuff already, but you didn't even know it's called instructional design until you picked up this book. Am I right?

When people ask me what I do or what I am a doctor of, my answer usually elicits a blank stare (or they shrug and walk away). If I go on to say "Instructional design is the science of building learning programs so people can process, retain and recall…" well, I don't even get to finish because they are long gone with that glazed over look on their faces.

Admit it, you just zoned out too, right? Instructional design isn't all that exciting to most people. I'm a nerd about it, but if you are reading this, chances are you are NOT a nerd for instructional design. Because if you were, you'd be reading something by Merrill or Van Morrenböer or Kirschner. Instead, you've picked up this little easy read and not an article about systematic four-component instructional design and blah blah blah.

Chances are, you are in HR or learning and development and you have been tasked with getting learning to the people, but you have no background in instructional design. The truth is, a large percentage of people in learning and development roles who are putting together learning for their organization have no idea what instructional design is, nor actually have experience in instructional design. Is that you?

How many times have you watched a YouTube video to learn, say, Excel functions? How boring was it? You learned what you needed to for that moment, but do you remember anything else about that video? No? And the reason is that the video didn't follow any instructional design principles and therefore you didn't process it, and you can't recall it. You do recall the small part of it that you applied right away though, right? And there's a reason for that as well. We'll get to that later. For now, know that knowing just a few of the basics about instructional design (we're not talking theory or anything heavy here, you dig?) will improve the way your people learn and ultimately benefit your business's bottom line as your people will learn and become faster and better.

I've been in the field of learning and development for over 20 years, consulting with companies around the globe. And one thing I've realized in all of the years I've been doing this is that most people who have been tasked with putting together learning programs have little or no experience or formal education in instructional design. Am I looking at you? You bet I am.

But to create learning experiences that people will use (meaning its engaging), retain (meaning its useful), and recall (meaning it connects) requires at least a basic understanding of some principles of instructional design.

So let's talk about how to use this book.

What do you know already? Are you familiar with learning in the flow of work? Skip chapter 2. Are you currently creating learning courses, videos, articles, case studies or other assets for your learners? You might want to read this whole thing, but you could start with Chapter 3. Are you implementing an LMS at your company and need to decide what to put it in? Start with Chapter 6.

Bottom line – use this book as you need to. I wrote it for you to have as a reference. Keep it on your desk, use those little sticky tabs on pages that you'll need to refer back to. And if you don't want to read from cover to cover, well then don't! It's meant as a reference book, not a novel. And no one's going to quiz you on the content.

So let's get started. Welcome to the wonderful world of Learning Experience Design.

2 - Formal Shmormal: The new way of learning

Formal learning is dead.
Wow, that's a bold statement isn't it? And it's not entirely true, I just wanted to get your attention. The truth is, learning is pragmatic. Formal learning – and by that, I mean classroom-based, PowerPoint pushing, assessment taking, locked down, "you have to do it this way" learning programs – still have their place. They just don't have THE place they used to have.

They should be used rarely, selectively, and after exhausting all other options for learning. Why? Because they are limited in effectiveness. They produce a lot of scrap learning. People go into that room, take in all kinds of information, and then only retain about 20% of it over the next few weeks (so the rest of the stuff they learned is scrapped, thus "scrap learning"- get it?) So you could say that formal learning is kinda wasteful, right? Especially compared to someone taking a shorter course, online, at their desk, and applying it right away, why take them away from that and into a classroom? It just doesn't make sense anymore.

Part of the reason that classroom learning is no longer the way to go is because the nature of learning has changed over the years. We used to think that it was a good idea to take people out of their work environment so they could focus on learning new skills and concept. We've now come to realize that when we do that, they lose 80% of that learning in six weeks. Why? Because they don't apply it. You've likely seen the Ebbinghaus Curve recently, showing that as we get further away from a learning experience, we lose more and more of what we learned unless it is reinforced. (Figure 2.1) Over the years, we've come to learn that what we call "formal learning", or putting people into a formal setting for 8 hours of talking to them, just is not effective. Not only is it not effective, but it wastes an awful lot of money.

Figure 2.1: Ebbinghaus Forgetting Curve

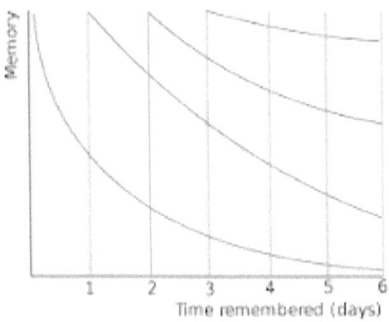

I did a project with a company years ago in which we revamped their new hire training. The original new hire training for sales reps was a 6-week program during which they flew everyone into their corporate training center from all over the country and put them in a hotel for 6 weeks while they pushed PowerPoint at them for 5 weeks. Then they put them in a workshop for a week to apply what they had learned. After all of that time and money, 60% of those new hires quit after the first few months. Mainly because they had not retained the vital information we had taught them about the products that was necessary to make sales. Way too much scrap learning there, let me tell ya. Way.Too.Much.

We rebuilt that program to 4 weeks of online learning during which they did field experience. Then we mixed in 1 week of time in the classroom/workshop. We saved them over $1 million a year in training and opportunity costs. I know. It doesn't seem like all that much now, but we're talking 20 years ago. And the retention rate of new hires went up to 80%. It wasn't hard to revamp that program, we just had to think about it from a different point of view and get away from the formal learning mindset.

If you haven't got my point already, here it is: Formal, classroom-based training is no longer the way to go. It's not very effective or efficient for the day-to-day learning that needs to happen in today's corporate environment.

The New Lingo

Before we get very far, there are a few concepts that you should know. In your travels around the world of learning and development, you may have heard certain old-school terms thrown around like "asynchronous learning", "synchronous learning", "virtual classroom" and "adult learning theory." Forget these terms (we'll actually talk about adult learning theory later.) Those are some old school terms and although they do have some important principles behind them, you need to understand more updated and relevant concepts.

There are new ways of learning that are better than the old-school formal stuff and there are new terms to go with them. Let's talk about microlearning, learning in the flow of work, continuous learning, and learning agility. This is the new, better way of learning for adults.

Microlearning

Chances are you've heard this one over the past couple of years. Or else you're working under a rock. Microlearning is the new buzz word in training and development. And it is exactly what it sounds like – micro, or very small, pieces of learning. The beauty of microlearning is that you can quickly gain a little piece of knowledge as you go about your day. Maybe a 5-minute video on how to communicate with co-workers or a 2-minute book summary giving you the main points of the hottest leadership book released in the last year. Microlearning makes learning in the flow of work possible. We'll get to that in a minute.

But first, let's address a misconception about microlearning. You might have heard the doubters say it's no good because people need more. They need context. They need to build knowledge one piece at a time. They say microlearning only gives learners a small piece of information. To those doubters I say, read this book and you'll know how to use microlearning correctly!

The thing is, you can't take one microlearning asset and expect to know all you need to know. The point of microlearning is that you can take one small piece at a time, process that one part in your brain before you then get another piece of information and process that one. It's like that diet where they say you should eat every hour. A little nibble here, a little nibble there... but instead of losing weight, you're gaining knowledge. And the way to make that work is by incorporating the principle of learning in the flow of work.

Learning in the flow of work

As we've discussed already, learning at work used to be a highly formal process. We would take months, we're talking six to eight months, to create PowerPoints, instructor guides and participant guides. We would schedule days or weeks for people to fly somewhere to have those PowerPoints pushed at them while they took notes (or not) in the participant guides. Then we'd fly everyone back to their offices and expect that they would then apply that knowledge on the job. And they'd lose 80% of it by the time a month went by. Well, that was a waste of time (eye roll.)

But we're getting a lot better at understanding

how people should learn to make it effective and efficient. Learning in the flow of work is the way to do that. It's a concept introduced by Josh Bersin in research for Bersin by Deloitte. It makes a lot more sense than that formal learning we used to do. Because learning in the flow of work means you are getting what you need when you need it and applying it immediately. So you don't lose it.

At its core, learning in the flow of work is going through your day and learning while you do. A mentoring session with your manager is learning. Clicking the Help button in PowerPoint so you can figure out how to create an animation is learning. Reading a book summary on your phone while you slam down your lunch sandwich at your desk is learning. And these activities are all a part of your day, right? Then you add in a few learning assets that are pushed to you – like a link to a video in an email or a course module related to a core company competency, and suddenly you are learning and growing as you work. So that's learning in the flow of work. Make sense? Now, let's not confuse learning in the flow of work with continuous learning, as many people do.

Continuous learning

Continuous learning is tied to learning in the flow of work. Many people in learning and development use them synonymously. But they're not the same. Where learning in the flow of work is about taking small nuggets of knowledge and applying them immediately to whatever you're doing during your day, continuous learning is about constant, vigilant improvement. Continuous learning means that you are always, always, always learning and never stop. As kids, every single thing you do is a learning experience. You see new things all the time, and your little spongy brain takes it all in and gains knowledge constantly.

As we get older, we already know what an apple is and how to drive a car, so learning new things is rare. Learning experiences are fewer and farther between. The Japanese have a word: Shoshin, or "beginners mind." It means to continue to improve, to continue to learn. Although less and less experiences are learning experiences as an adult, there are still very many experiences you have in a day that teach you something! A conversation with a co-worker, a mentoring session, a magazine article that you picked up, a short video that intrigued you on social media. All of these things are examples of learning assets. Truly, you are learning continuously.

Okay, so we're always learning, and that's what continuous learning means. But, you ask, what does that have to do with my role in learning and development (or whatever it may be, related to learning in the corporate world)? Well, it's up to you to ensure your people have the opportunities for continuous learning. We'll cover more of that later. Meanwhile, let's chat about……

Learning agility

Again, you may have heard this term used in conjunction with or synonymous to continuous learning. But the difference between them is a nuance. You've likely heard the term agility thrown around a lot these days. There's an Agile method for project management, companies need to be agile, agility is important for corporate growth, etc, etc, etc. Learning agility is similar. Rather than being about learning in the flow of work or learning continuously, learning agility is about constantly ensuring you are changing up what you are learning so that it's relevant to today. Learning agility is the ability to pivot, to change your mind, to un-learn what you thought was true and find a new, better truth.

What I mean is this:

As you know, and as I've mentioned many times already, we live in a constantly changing world. Things keep moving faster and faster, and companies (and people) need to keep learning in order to keep up. There's always some new way of doing something or some research showing new findings that we didn't know before (didn't they once believe that Earth was flat?) or a different point of view that opens up new possibilities for understanding the world (why isn't Pluto a planet anymore, again?) Things change. A LOT. And if you want to keep up with the world and you want your people to know how to keep up with the world, you have to have and promote learning agility. You have to stay on top of what the newest information is and ensure that your people have access to it so they can learn continuously. Are you seeing the nuances of continuous learning versus learning agility yet?

Here's an example:

You can talk with your executives and management and find out that your company needs leadership training. So you do your research and find a great program that meets all of your needs for leadership readiness. Awesome! All set, right? You go ahead and spend your entire budget on this amazing program that's going to ensure your company has a great ascension program for your future leaders and you're gonna use it for the next 5-10 years to build your leadership pipeline. Awesome!

But wait! Three months down the line, you see research that shows that the old way of preparing leaders is no longer valid, and that there is a better way to prepare your leaders for their ascension up the corporate ladder. There are all kinds of new programs out there that subscribe to this new research, and it's been shown to be more effective than the old way. So, what now?

Pivot. Change it up, however you need to do that. The key to learning agility is to be prepared for the unexpected. So instead of spending your entire leadership budget on a single program from the get-go, you know that it will likely change, so you keep something in reserve. Make sense?

Learning agility as a culture means you are always ready to change. You cannot put learning out there and just let it be. Learning agility means you stay on top of our ever-changing world and update your microlearning and continuous learning to match. Being agile means being able to change at the drop of a hat or the turn of information. You're able to pivot with any new information. Learning agility means you are able to change up what you are doing quickly, as new information appears. We'll talk more about how to do this later. But now, let's cover what these new terms mean for the way we deliver learning to our people.

New ways of learning, new roles for L&D

Learning in the flow of work describes the new direction of instructional design. Where instructional design used to be about creating these formal learning courses, we're now moving to a direction where it's more about compiling good learning using existing resources mixed with custom built resources. It's more about designing learning experiences than creating instruction. Because let's face it, there is a plethora of content out there already. If you need to learn something, you can pretty much find a video or book or website related to that topic. Ted Talks, YouTube, online journals, presentations, web pages, case studies… just to name a few. There is so much content out there! You don't really need to create a lot. BUT, you do need to put it together in a meaningful way. And you need to be able to discern good content from bad. You don't want to just throw any old information out there for your people, right? So how do you ensure the content is good and that you are putting it together in a meaningful way? That's what we're here to talk about.

To put together or create learning that is sticky (meaning it's useful to your audience) you need

to have three things:
1. An understanding of their needs,
2. Content that meets their needs, and
3. A learning environment that is easy to access and use.

Seems simple, right? And it is, once you understand the best ways to get each of those three things.

Do you know how often your audience is Googling something while at work, or how many YouTube videos they have watched to learn some simple Excel function or Word procedure? A lot. That's how often. And the reason is because it's easy, it's relevant, and it's what they need when they need it.

But the thing is, how much time did they waste on that Google search, and how many videos did they have to sift through that were not relevant or useful before they finally found the right one? Again, a lot. That's how many.

Thus, the role of L&D is changing. Where we used to design learning for people, now we need to curate learning for our people. We need to help our people find those relevant videos and other, better content sources) faster. Our job is to ensure our people have access to what they need, quickly and easily, and that it is aligned to their needs and the needs of the company. Our job is no longer as an instructional design, but an experience designer. In the next chapter we'll talk about what that means.

3 – What the heck is Learning Experience Design?

I don't care what your current title is - whether you are an HR professional, the Director of Learning and Development, or a Sales Manager who just needs to get some good knowledge to your folks. You might even be a teacher! Whatever your job is, if you picked up this book, it's likely because you are doing some kind of learning design. You need to know best practices for making your people learn. You need to put together learning experiences, so you are a Learning Experience Designer.

Let's chat a bit about what that means. What exactly are learning experiences? Learning Experience Design is a pretty new concept. What we used to call Instructional Design is morphing into Experience Design, and that's because the nature of business has changed. The Digital Transformation, the need to keep up with the competition, the need to move quickly in business drives the need for learning to be available all the time, quickly, and when it's needed. Learning in the flow of work means that what you need to offer to your people are not the hour-long elearning courses or the eight-hour classroom courses. Those types of learning do require a thorough understanding of instructional design, because you have to create them using instructional design principles in order for them to be effective (and reduce, as much as possible, the scrap learning.)

If you are, in fact, an instructional designer you may now be saying to yourself (but really directed at me), "Wh-What? You're crazy, lady, you need instructional design!" Rest assured, you are still needed (and geez, I hope so because I spent a lot of time and energy working on a PhD in ID!). We still have a need for those one-hour elearning courses sometimes, and even the instructor-led training is still, on occasion, the perfect way to go. And later in a later chapter we're going to talk about when you need to "build it". But what we're talking about here is the "microlearning in the flow of work" stuff. That's a learning experience, not an elearning course. And it does require some level of understanding of ID, just not a full-on education in ID. That's why we're here, right?

Back to learning experiences. What I mean by that is the whole experience around learning at work. How do you want your people to learn continuously? What should learning look like in your organization if people are truly learning continuously and in the flow of work? I'll wait a minute while you get a vision in your head.

Okay, ready to go on? Here's my vision for a day in the life of an employee in an organization that is truly promoting continuous learning and allowing for learning in the flow.

A day in the life of a corporate learner

Charlie walks into work and sits at her desk. When she boots up the computer, the company Intranet site pops up with a message that reads "Today's video is ready for your viewing. Would you like to view it now?" Charlie clicks OK (or taps on "View later" and she gets a reminder at noon) and a 2-minute video on communication skills plays. This video shows an example of what good communication skills look like in a scenario similar to her work so Charlie can connect it to her day and use it immediately. It is also related to the mission of the organization which includes exceptional customer service. After Charlie watches the short video, she gets on with her day. She's opening emails and after deleting the 15 spam emails in her inbox, she comes across one from her manager reminding her that they have a 2 PM meeting to write her goals for the year, and that she needs to have 3 SMART goals written for the meeting. The email contains a link to a section of a course in the learning system that reminds her how to do SMART goals. She clicks it, goes through a 5-minute module about how to create SMART goals, then writes the three she needs for her meeting with her manager.

At 11 AM a reminder pops up in Outlook that she needs to continue working through her leadership learning program. The reminder contains links to each of the assets that are a part of the leadership program she is working through. She clicks on the one for today and reads a summary of *Turn the Ship Around* by L. David Marquet. She then goes back to the Outlook calendar item and answers three questions about the summary that apply it to her organization.

After lunch (a salad from Panera at her desk, sound familiar?) she begins to work on a project that is next on her to-do list. She needs to analyze some data in Excel for a client, but she can't remember how to do a vLookup. She clicks on the vLookup function in Excel, then clicks the question mark that pops up, and her learning system serves up a quick how-to video showing her how to complete a vLookup right on top of her Excel window. She watches the 1-minute video then closes it and resumes her work in Excel.

AT 2 PM she meets with her manager for a mentoring session and to set up her SMART goals. As they talk, her manager logs their main discussion points into the learning system, and notes where Charlie has grown in the past 3 months since their last meeting. This is learning, too!

Her day goes on like this – learning constantly, all day long, without interrupting her work to leave for a classroom session or stop working for an hour to take an online course or read a book chapter.

As adults, we need to learn constantly and apply what we learn as we go. As Experience Designers, it is up to you to promote that learning and provide easy ways for your people to be exposed it.

So now that you get the idea, what is your vision for experience design at your company? Is it different than it was before reading about Charlie's day? Think about how your company can support the continuous learning culture and how you can design the experiences to fit that culture.

Types of microlearning

Now that you have a clearer understanding of microlearning and Learning Experience Design let's talk a bit about the guts of it. Learning experience design is the process of putting together pieces of microlearning so that you cover an entire topic. It's also how the learner accesses those assets throughout their day, but we'll get to that part later. The first step is figuring out what you can offer. Microlearning can take many formats. Here are just a few:

- *Video*: Microlearning videos are short and to the point. They should really be "sweet" also, meaning that they are engaging so people want to watch them. Short videos means no longer than about 5 minutes. The exact perfect time would be 3 minutes, as that gives you time to get the point across quickly but doesn't give time to get into too many extraneous details.
    a. You can have talking head videos, where it's an expert sitting in a chair (pipe and smoking jacket are optional) talking to you about whatever subject he's an expert at.
    b. You can have whiteboard videos – the kind with a hand drawing and erasing stuff on a whiteboard as a narrator discusses a topic.
    c. You can have marketing-type videos, with images and text flying at you while music plays.

Certainly, there are many other types out there. The key is that they are short, that's what makes them microlearning

- *Books*: Clearly an entire book would not be considered microlearning, as it would take much longer than a few minutes to read. Book chapters, book summaries, a few pages - these would be considered microlearning. Remember it needs to be short, ideally taking about 5 to 10 minutes to read. (Note that this is simply a guideline for book chapters and summaries, as everyone reads at a different pace.)
- *Online Writing*: Blogs, online articles, web sites or pages from experts, and case studies can all be considered microlearning. After all, when you read them you learn something, right? A link to a website or blog can usually be added to a learning system as a learning object, so you can track it and consider it part of a learning experience.
- *Casual (or formal) Meetings*: Mentoring sessions, meetings with a manager or co-worker that share knowledge, cohort groups and other types of interactions are actually types of microlearning. You could have an online discussion group that is brainstorming the best ways to have an agile frame of mind, or a cohort group that meets at the watercooler once a week for 15 minutes to discuss the advantages of a diverse workplace. These are all types of learning experiences, and they are short… so, microlearning!
- *Course modules/lessons*: This is probably the most obvious type of microlearning to most people. A section of a longer course – a lesson that is 5 minutes or less is definitely microlearning. Most

pre-packaged courses these days are created using shorter lessons all packaged into a single course so that you can take either the whole thing (giving full context) or just a single part that is relevant to what you need.

Learning Experience Design, though, is much more than stringing together pieces of microlearning. It's also ensuring that the pieces are easy to get to, can be tracked and are relevant to the users. It's about the end-to-end experience of learning continuously, in the flow of work. To be able to create these great learning experiences for people, there are some principles of instructional design that you should have some basic understanding of.

4 – What we adults like

Do you remember when I mentioned scrap learning a few times in the previous chapters? There are ways of doing things that make learning more, or less, effective (If you skipped over the scrap learning part, you can find it in Chapter 2.) Instructional designers do certain things when they create learning courses or programs and much of the reason they do those certain things is to reduce scrap learning. They want to make learning effective and efficient. And even though we're not really talking about pure instructional design here, there are some principles that Experience Designers need to understand in order to make the learning experiences stick. Especially when it comes to creating learning experiences for adults.

Teaching adults is very different from teaching kids. Many of us started out as teachers and ended up as instructional designers, which is ironic isn't it? But as teachers, we had little training in instructional design. We learned it as we went by creating lesson plans for our classes. But working with adults is very different. Very different indeed! We as adult have very specific things we like if we are to learn something new.

There are some basic principles about the way adults learn that will help you to get good learning to your people. They are:
- Relevance
- Emotion
- Self-direction
- Experience

Now, if you go researching the adult learning theory or andragogy, you're going to find a whole lot more than those four little words. There are actually five assumptions and four principles related to adult learning theory. But I've simplified it a bit for you. If you really want to dig deeper into adult learning theory, look up Malcolm Knowles. He's the guy who realized that adults learn differently than kids do, and he developed the idea of andragogy or adult learning theory.

For our purposes in this book, I'm just giving you the basics that will help you to create great learning experiences for your folks. These four areas will help you to better understand where your audience is coming from (figuratively speaking) so you can create learning experiences that reduce scrap learning.

Relevance

We adults learn best when we can quickly tie the knowledge to something in real life. The key here is "quickly." If I read something today and then don't use that knowledge for a month or so, guess what? It's gone. Scrapped. History. Outta there. It was time wasted – because my brain won't hold onto it if I don't use it quickly or connect it to something. It's like your brain is going, "Hey, there's enough useless junk in here. What do I need that piece of information for if it's not useful? Forget it man!"

Think about something you watched on YouTube a month ago. Just any old random thing that wasn't related to something in your life or work. Do you remember all those random videos and memes that you stayed up late watching last week? Of course not. Maybe you can remember the one with the dog who got into the trash and ended up with the trash can lid around his neck. And that's not relevant to your work or life, you say. True. But it connected to something in your mind, and that's why you remember it. It was also emotional because it made you laugh, but we'll get to that in a minute.

Our brains are like giant databases. They are the biggest computers ever! ENIAK had nothing on the human brain. We can store so much more data than you ever thought possible. But in order to recall that data, it needs to be connected to something. It needs to be relevant to our life or our work. That's what makes us remember it.

My point here is that if you want people to get something from the learning that you put out there for them, it has to be relevant to their life and work. They need to use it right away, connect with it or apply it somehow to their life. Use it or lose it.

Emotion

Let's go back to that video of the dog. No, it wasn't relevant, and no you didn't apply anything so you'd remember it. So why did you remember it? Why is it still in your craw?

If you're not familiar with the video I'm referencing here's a synopsis:
>A man comes home from work to find a trashcan knocked over and trash

everywhere. There are three dogs that are the suspects. After walking toward them with their very contrite looks, he comes across Tank, with the trash can lid around his neck.

The reason you remember this particular video (if you saw it) is because you connected with it. It's real life. If you've had a dog in your life, you can imagine this happening. If you've never had a pupper, you at least have known someone who has and can imagine this going down. And it's funny.

The pupper had the trash can lid around his neck and was looking pretty contrite about the whole "Who got into the trash?" thing, right? It was funny, and you connected with it on an emotional level. Your brain will take that emotional connection and remember it. But if you're one of the people who is right now reading this and thinking "Eh, not all that funny" then you wouldn't remember it even if you did see it. That's just how our brains work. If it's not emotional to you and not relevant, your brain automatically dismisses it.

Think about a memory from when you were a kid. Was there emotion in that memory? Likely, yes, whether you recognize it or not. When we have strong emotions around something, we are much more likely to process it and recall it later.

Your learners, your audience, need to connect to the learning somehow. A PowerPoint with bullet points isn't going to bring out any emotion and frankly they'll forget it pretty quickly (if they even bother to read it at all.) But an image on that PowerPoint showing people who are similar to those they work with will bring some emotion and relevance to that information and they will connect with it and store it for recall later.

Imagine you are reading a book about leadership. And this book lists all the skills you need and even tells you how to gain those skills. You can apply each of those skills as soon as you read it, and that's one way to get learners to remember it. But, you can also add stories that might provoke an emotional response and have the reader connect. They'll remember it then, too.

So when you're thinking about putting great learning out there for your audience, no matter if you build it, find it, or buy it, you'll want to ensure it connects with your audience on an emotional level. That's the second adult learning principle.

Self-direction

I don't know about you, but I don't like to be told

what to do. As an adult, this also applies to learning. I don't like to be told what to learn. I mean, most of us don't, right? So why do we tell other adults what they need to know?

Adults like to take responsibility of their own learning. Telling them "Here, go learn this" just isn't going to work with them. Would that approach work for you? I didn't think so.

Self-direction also applies to how adults learn. They (and by "they" I mean "we") like to explore. We want to be able to take control of what we are learning and doing. An online course that forces us to go through every single page and read every piece of text is, quite frankly, going to piss us off. I'm going to just get mad and let the thing run through so I can get credit for it without every actually watching any of it, right? But if I can control how quickly I can move forward and I can decide to skip over sections because I already know that information, then I'm in control and I'm much happier.

The same holds true for books. I had a high school English teacher in my senior year who told me that there was no reason to read every single word in a book. It blew my mind! As a child, we're taught to read every word, right? But as adults (and as a high school senior I was on the cusp of adulthood, or so I thought), he told us we could be in control of our own learning. And he was right! Sometimes I just read the topic sentence of a paragraph and learn all I need to know. And that's my choice, as an adult learner. I want to be in control of my learning.

Yessiree, we adult learners like to learn our own way. This is one of the reasons continuous learning or learning in the flow of work is such a great approach. We put the knowledge assets out there for people to use, and they find what they need and consume them at their own pace. Self-direction is important for adult learners, so why not allow them to have it?

Experience

Adults come to work with a vast array of experiences. Obviously, since they've been on this earth for a bit – some much more than others. They don't want to waste their time on learning something they already know. So consider your audience when pushing out learning. Do they need a basic level of knowledge, or a more advanced understanding?
Think about something you read or learned recently. Did you pay attention to every word? No? Because some of it was review for you, right?

You already knew this or that, so no need to relearn it. Now imagine sitting down to read a book that you think is going to help you get ahead in your job. You start reading and the first chapter is all things you already know. Will you continue? Nope, skip that chapter. On to Chapter 2. Same thing – boring, I already know this. On to Chapter 3… same thing. I already know this. So now I just wasted maybe 30 minutes reading things I already know. And I'm done with that book. If Chapter 4 is useful, I'll never know. It took me too long to get there so I gave up.

When compiling videos, books and courses, take the learner's experience into consideration. Don't insult them with content that's too basic. But also don't give them content that's too deep for what they need. That would be as much a waste of time as the basic stuff. The key is to provide a variety of levels of content to meet everyone's needs, and allow them to pick and choose what's relevant to their experience. How? We'll get to this later. For now, remember that adults have life experience. They have existing knowledge and if you try to give them learning experiences that waste their time or don't account for their existing knowledge, they're going to get bored or frustrated and not bother.

Creating learning experiences for adults is very different than creating learning for kids or teens. Adults have specific needs, so ensure that whatever you are providing them respects andragogy. It needs to be relevant to their needs, connect with them emotionally, allow them to be in control, and acknowledge that they already have experience.

5 – Who you talkin' to?

Now let's talk about that audience of yours. Every audience is different. Every audience has different needs, but all people need to learn to keep growing and improving. They need to gain knowledge for many reasons – to do a new task, to improve the way they do a task, to gain a new skill or improve upon an existing skill, to do their job better, to get a new job, to get promoted – and a myriad of other reasons. And in today's rapidly changing environment, they need to learn quickly. But how do you know what they need to learn so you can get them the learning quickly?

In instructional design terms, you do a needs analysis. For IDs this is often a pretty formal process of meeting with various business line owners, or other stakeholders and managers, and walking through a pretty extensive questionnaire. But once again, that's the old-world way of doing it. We no longer have time for an extensive needs analysis. And we no longer need to be so formal. Just like learning in the flow of work, you should continuously be assessing the needs of your audiences and continuously updating the learning available to them so they can keep learning and moving up or forward.

So how do you constantly analyze your audience to always know what the newest thing is they need to learn? Here are a few ways:

Hanging at the Watercooler

Just ask when you are standing around the watercooler (literally or figuratively). "Hey, I was wondering – what learning would you like to see out there?" You'll get a few answers, or maybe you won't. But it's worth an ask, because this is a place where you'll see all kinds of people and many who you don't necessarily interact with in your normal day-to-day operations. What I'm really saying here is to ask everyone what they need, and ask them often. Doing this will help you to keep an eye on the pulse of the audiences you serve and their needs.

But don't just ask for a list of what they need. Make sure you also ask "Why?" Some people may tell you they need learning on a specific skill or topic when what they really need is something else. Huh? Here's what I mean:

> You ask Bob what he needs to learn. He says "Everyone in my department needs to learn about project management." So you go off and buy a bunch of online videos about project management and how to manage projects from start to finish. Good, done. Bob should be all set.
>
> But a month later you go into your LMS reporting and see that Bob, and everyone else in Bob's department, hasn't been using those videos. What's up with that? So the next day at the watercolor (or on Jabber, or in the Starbucks line, or wherever you see Bob) you casually ask Bob why he hasn't been watching the videos on project management that he asked you for.
>
> He says "They don't count for PMI certification. My people need courses that they can use to get certified by the Project Management Institute. We already know how to do project management. We need the more

advanced stuff that will get us certified." Yikes. Bob has 500 people across the globe that do project management under him. You just wasted an awful lot of time and capital because of one little word. Why?

What's our lesson here? Constantly, informally check in with people and ask what they want or need to learn. When you're at the watercooler, in the hallway, at the cafeteria, chatting via email, on a Webex, at the Starbucks in the lobby ask ask ask. Stay on top of what the people want. But don't rush out to get them content to meet those needs until you've asked "Why?" and dug a little deeper into exactly what it is they need.

Manager Chats

Good managers – lets face it, not all managers are good managers – will have an eye on what their people need to grow and improve. Talk to them often. Call them up or set up a meeting with them monthly to discuss their people needs. This type of meeting is best done either face-to-face or phone-to-phone, in real time. Emailing to ask a manager what her people needs rarely yields good results. Trust me on that.

Good people managers are continually trying to grow their people. They may have a list of skills or knowledge that they have discussed with their people and know they need to learn. They might have a career growth plan for their direct reports with learning needs clearly defined. Maybe they have a formal learning plan in place already and need content to fill it. Managers who are trying to grow their people are definitely a great place to find out what is needed for learning in your company. So talk to them regularly.

Listen, Listen, Listen

This is the method where you just keep your eyes and ears open at all times, everywhere you are. Listen. Employees talk all the time. I don't mean just in the office, because many of us work from home-based offices or are on the road all the time. Check emails, chat logs, phone call notes. Listen to what people are saying in Webex meetings, or what you hear at the coffee counter. People will often let you know what they need in an off-handed way.

"Man, I was really having trouble figuring out how to set up that PowerPoint."

"The other day it took me 3 hours just to understand what this guy was trying to tell me!"

"My manager is awful. She never tells me

anything. I could do her job so much better!"

From just those 3 statements, it sounds like these people need training in PowerPoint, some learning about communication skills, and maybe some leadership programs. Do you see that?

Note that I'm not suggesting that every time someone tells you their needs or complains about not knowing how to do something that you should run out to buy some learning assets for them! Instead, paying attention to the people around you, those you serve as your audience, will begin to show patterns of what's needed.

Here's an example.

You overheard a co-worker say something about his manager wanting to hire some new people while you were in line at the coffee shop. You hadn't heard that anyone was hiring, but it's a big company so whatever, right? Then you're walking to a meeting with another colleague and she tells you she heard the IT department is looking for people with CompTIA certifications. You get an email from HR asking for referrals for CompTIA certified people. You were called into a meeting last week to brainstorm ideas for how the company can be more digitally native, and you learned in that meeting that the execs at the company want to ensure you stay competitive by implementing new technologies and changing the way things are done for your customers.

There's a lot of information there that you can put together to understand some of the learning needs at your company. You might want to consider CompTIA certification for existing IT employees. Maybe some content on digital transformation. Perhaps a new hire orientation program. The thing is, you figured that out just from listening to what was going on around you. You can then take those thoughts to management or the exec team and say "Hey, it seems like maybe we need some learning in digital transformation, is that what you're thinking too?"

Another way of using the listen, listen, listen method is to listen to other HR or learning and development groups to see what they are doing. Know someone in HR at another company? Call him and ask him what the hot learning is at his company. Go to learning and development conferences – there are literally thousands of them every year, from huge Training Magazine week-long extravaganzas to small local events with 25 people. Check them out, attend them, get ideas. Also, read, read, read! Industry magazines will give you tons of ideas about what the trending training topics are (leading for the digital age, anyone?) not to mention pointing you to some places to buy, beg or build (we'll get to that soon).

Talent Management System, obviously

If your company has a formal process for evaluation and promotion, this is an invaluable tool for you to find out what people need to know in order to grow. I feel silly even telling you this because it's really a no-brainer, right? But I put it out here just to remind you of all the ways you can figure out what folks need.

What I mean by saying "use your talent management system" is that this is a place where a plethora of information is stored about what folks need to know to move into their next role or improve in their current role. If the system is within your ownership then great! You're all set. Pull some reports and start finding content to match! If it's not in your area of responsibility, it's time to make friends with whoever does own it so you can get what you need.

Mission, Vision and Competencies

Another avenue to find what is needed is by using your company's mission statement, vision statement, and competency framework, if your company has any or all of these. Let's talk mission and vision first.

Using the mission and vision isn't quite as simple as the first few methods I discussed earlier, but it is something you should keep on your radar. It's what drives everything your company does and the direction you're headed so it's imperative that you have at least some understanding of it to ensure you are aligning learning assets to it. The way to do this is to review the mission statement and the vision (although the mission typically is more action-oriented) to find key words that are actionable. Then you want to align content areas that will help drive the company toward that mission.

Let's look at some examples of how to do this.

Here's the mission statement from Prezi (the company that creates the Prezi software):
To reinvent how people share knowledge, tell stories, and inspire their audiences to act.

Read that statement again. Do you see some actionable areas jumping out at you?
Read it again. And again.

Now do you see some? I'll share with you what I saw.

"Reinvent how people share knowledge": If you're going to reinvent something you need to be innovative, right? You can't reinvent anything without innovation. Do your people know how to be innovative? Maybe some of them. But this is definitely an area where you'd want to have learning assets. Innovation.

"Share knowledge": What do you need to be able to do if you want to share knowledge? Do you need to know how to communicate effectively, yes? Of course you do! You can't just go yell at people and expect them to share in your knowledge. So there's a second area of focus from the mission statement – Communication skills.

Last one I see. Do you see it? One more area in that mission statement that stands out as an area that we could provide some learning. How about "Inspire their audiences to act?" What kinds of skills would you need to be able to inspire people to act? Did you say "leadership?" Of course you did. Because yes! Inspiring people means leading them. We need to make sure the folks at Prezi have some good leadership skills in order to inspire others.
Let's take a look at another example.
Everybody loves Southwest Airlines, even if you've never flown. So let's see what the mission of this fun airline is. "The mission of Southwest Airlines is dedication to the highest quality of

customer service delivered with a sense of warmth, friendliness, individual pride, and company spirit."

Alright, so let's take another minute here. What are some areas of learning that this mission statement defines for us? Well the first is obvious, I think. Did you catch it? That's right, customer service. That one sort of just shoots right out at you, doesn't it?

What else do you see in this mission statement? How do you develop a sense of warmth and friendliness? There is a specific skill set that would help you to be more warm and friendly to others. People skills. Working with people, interacting with people, communicating with warmth and kindness. These are all skills that can be taught to help your people develop a sense of warmth and friendliness.

Individual pride is not quite as easy to figure out. But again, books, videos and other content that is about building self-esteem or building self-confidence should help people with the pride thing. If people love what they do, they tend to be proud of what they do. Offering learning programs that are about how great the company is, how great their job is – these will help to give people that sense of individual pride.

Another way to figure out what learning is needed to help drive the mission statement is to talk to the company executives. I know this is not always an option, especially in some really big companies. But if you can, talk to the executives who wrote the mission statement. Or, talk to execs who didn't write the mission statement but are who working to drive the mission of the company. Those are the people who should know what the mission statement means. They should have a deep understanding of how to apply it at your company, so they will be able to break it down to help you understand what learning needs to be offered to drive that mission.

With all mission statements, it's best to talk to people in the know about what is meant them. Certain things, like customer service, are obvious. But others are not so much. So talk to people who can help you understand those statements at a deeper level and break it down a bit more. Ask "What does someone who _____ (e.g. has individual pride) do differently?" Once you know the answer to that, you can align learning assets to meet that need.

Back to your audience. Many companies will put lots of learning out there (ie: on their learning system) without every listening to what's needed or thinking about aligning to competencies. They make assumptions that all companies need learning related to leadership and communication skills and project management. And that's fine, if you want to be average. But to truly have great learning, you need to understand your audience and give them what they need. Think about who you're talking to (figuratively, of course) and cater the learning to their needs. Now, how do you get that learning that fits those needs? Let's talk about that in Chapter 6.

6 – Beg, buy or build

Designing learning experiences is putting together a complex puzzle, but without having the benefit of the picture on the box or the pieces all rattling around inside. You have to first decide what picture the picture looks like, then find the pieces that fit together to make the picture whole, then you have to put them together in a way that makes sense to the learner, and not necessarily to you. Have you ever seen an impressionist painting made of dots, like a Monet? Think about what it took for him to put all those dots in the exact right place so that when you looked at it, it appeared as a picture and not just a bunch of dots on a canvas. You are Dali. Your audience are the art critics. How do you put it together? It's a little bit science, a little bit art. Let's look at how to do that.

You understand your audience's needs. That's the picture that you have to work with. Now you need to find the pieces that will allow people to put the puzzle together. They can't put the full puzzle in place without all the pieces, right? How many times have you tried to finish a puzzle only to find that 2 to 3 pieces were missing? That's frustrating. You don't want your people to go through that. You want them to have all the pieces they need to learn whatever it is you are helping them to learn. You want to acquire all the microlearning pieces that can flow together to cover whatever a full elearning course or 8-hour classroom course would have, only better, faster, and cheaper.

So to get those pieces of microlearning that you will build into a learning experience for your people, you can beg for them, buy them or build them.

Many learning and development people immediately go to "build". Some immediately go to "buy". The smaller ones with no budget stick in the "beg" area. But the best in class learning programs contain a little bit of each. Variety is the spice of life, as they say, and this is especially true of learning experiences. Everyone has their best way to learn. For some of us, we remember things we write (I still remember a phone number from 1972 because I wrote it down once.) For some of us, we hear it and never forget it (like my friend who is always correcting me when I sing the wrong lyrics to any song). Still others need to see the printed word (how about that friend who has to put the sub-titles on every time you watch a movie?) And there are those who have to actually DO something to learn it (I know someone who always says "Let's try it and see what happens!") To meet the needs of all your audience members, you need to have some of all of these. Read, watch, listen, and apply.

The main point I want to get across here is that you don't need to buy a program. And if you do buy a program, most likely it will fit maybe 75-80% of your needs, max. When you buy a program or curriculum, you're buying sort of a generic curricula; one that is not exactly the perfect fit for your program, but is pretty close. With the knowledge you're gaining in this little book, you can easily put together a program that 100% fits the needs of your people – and you do that by begging for (ie: finding) some assets, buying some assets and building some assets. Then you put together those assets into an amazing learning experience that your people can take in the flow of work, at their own pace, when they need it, so it's relevant and useful.

Now, let's talk a bit about how you do that. Not all content assets will have titles that make it easy to know that they provide the knowledge you are seeking. In fact, many times you'll find that the title has nothing to do with what is being taught. But I'm getting ahead of myself. Alignment is not hard, but it will be a heck of a lot easier if you understand some basic concepts.

Instructional designers love to use the words "goals" and "objectives." Sometimes, they'll even string them together "goals and objectives" like they are some sort of important phrase the you have to know. Forget it. You don't need to worry about goals and objectives. Because truthfully, those things should be pretty obvious in any learning you beg for or buy.

Let's take this alignment thing one step at a time. You now have a solid understanding of some learning thing that your audience needs. You talked to Melinda when you were both early to a meeting last week and she mentioned that her direct reports are struggling to work well together. The company has recently reorganized (as if most companies don't do that annually, right?) and many of the teams, hers included, are struggling to figure out how to work together. So you asked around to some other managers and found that yup, indeed there seems to be a problem in the organization with all these new teams struggling to figure out how to work together. Aha, an identified need! What do you do with that information? Guess what? I'm going to help you figure that out.

There are three ways to get learning experiences that people can use in the flow of work:

Beg, buy or build.

And the way you determine what you need is to walk through each of them, one by one. You don't want to have to build because that is the lengthiest and most expensive way to get content. And we really don't have time for that if we're trying to move into continuous learning. But if you have to, you have to. Then we'll get really serious about instructional design! We'll get to that.

Beg

Let's start with begging for content. I don't mean literally beg, although sometimes you might need to. What I'm really talking about is freebies.

The very first thing you will want to do when you're ready to get some content related to whatever topic you need is to see what kind of free stuff is out there. Because I mean seriously, there is a TON of free content out there! Why pay for it if you don't need to? Of course, a ton of it (and I'm talkin' like 98%) is junk. Just totally awful content. Really, really, really bad. But if there are millions of pieces of content out on the internet and 98% of them are bad, that still leaves like, 40,000 pieces of good stuff out there at a minimum! And I'm sure there's more than two million pieces of content out there that constitute learning assets, whether formal or informal. So my point is, it's a good place to start. Because everyone likes free, right?

But geez, how do you dig through all of that content to find the good stuff? We call this "curating content", and I'm sure you've heard that term at some point. There are a few ways to curate the content, the free stuff.
First, social curation. People, your people in your company, are always online They are, whether you see that or not. They are always on YouTube and Facebook and Twitter. And those people share stuff like crazy. So start there. And if your learning system has a social component, then that's a great place to look also, because you can see what people like and dislike, which will help narrow what you try to find for them.

Second, traditional curation. Get out there and find it. Okay, so you've got Google up in front of you and you're ready to search the internet for content related to working in teams. You put in "working in teams" (and use the quotation marks. If you're not good with Boolean searching, you need to get better at it) and you get...... 7,000,000 results. Ugh. As if you have time to start looking through all of those! And I guarantee many of them aren't even anything related to what you need. But you know what you might never have noticed at the top of the Google screen? Juuuuust below the search box, where you can switch between All, News, Images... there it is - books and videos categories. Bingo! Now there's a good place to start.

Yes, I realize you are still going to get a lot more than you have time to look through. Switch to videos and you get about 32,000. If you start at the top, though, you'll get the most relevant. By the time you get to the 50th (if you have the patience to scroll that far) you'll likely be looking at stuff that's not so relevant anyway.

Here's how I do it: I start scrolling and reading the titles and descriptions. If I see something where I go "Hmmmm, maybe?" then I'll click on it. Give it about 4 seconds in to decide if I want to continue. If within 4 seconds it doesn't grab my attention and seem relevant, I hit the back button and continue on.

I mentioned alignment related to goals and objectives previously. This is what you need to know about that in order to find learning that aligns to your needs:

The old school way to define what a course was about was to explicitly list the objectives of the course. You may recall seeing a screen or slide in courses that looked like this:

By the end of this course, you will:
- Do this thing,
- This thing,
- This thing, and
- This thing.

But when we're talking about microlearning, you typically won't see that. There isn't time in a 3 to 5 minute learning asset to first list out what you will learn. So how, then, do we determine if the learning aligns to your people's needs?

First, you can check the title and description in the Google search you completed. Some learning items will be pretty obvious (or seem to be) like "Communicating with Executives in the Workplace." Well, if your need is that you are working on communication skills for individual contributors who need to communicate better with management, then this one looks like it might fit the bill. So take a minute or 2 to start watching it. After about 30 seconds this learning asset should clearly show you how it's going to teach someone what you are looking for them to know. If, 30 seconds in, you're not seeing how people will learn to better communicate with their managers, shut it down and move on. That's one way to align learning to needs.

Another way is to read the description in the Google search. Again, there should be something in there that makes you think "Hnmm, that might work." For example, say you are looking for some learning assets so that your people are more innovative – that's a somewhat popular topic. You see an asset in the top 15 of your search for which the description reads "John Q talks about innovation in the office." Does that sound like what you need? Maybe, but the one below it reads "Melissa R discusses the steps you need to take to come up with more innovative ideas at work." Which one sounds better? The John Q one doesn't really sound like he's telling you how to be more innovative (although it might, if you care to take the time to watch it) where the Melissa R one explicitly says it will give you the steps you need to be more innovative. I'd go with Melissa. Now, of course, once you watch it maybe it's nothing like what you need, but that's why you have to launch it and check out at least the first 20 to 30 seconds.

The bottom line is, there is no exact science to aligning microlearning to corporate needs when you are creating learning experiences that include freebies. Without clearly defined objectives up front, you have to be the one to determine what the objectives of the video or book chapter might be. You have to determine if what you read or watched will meet the needs of your people.

Now, you could spend literally days or weeks trying to find free, good internet content related to the topic you need. There is a new job emerging in many training functions called "Content Curators" where that's all they do. They spend their days in search of good content aligned to company needs, and they aggregate that content into groups that make it simple to find. Doesn't sound like what you want to do? Me either. I reached the end of the internet one time many years ago and I don't really care to do it again. Luckily, if you don't have a content curator and you don't want to reach the end of the internet, you have some other choices. So, spend some time on it. Spend however much time you feel is appropriate. That amount of time is going to be directly proportionate to the amount of money you have to spend. Less money to spend = more time searching for free stuff. Amiright? When you're done finding what you can, or just plain old sick of looking, let's get on to buying.

Buy

Anything you want is out there, if you just have the money. All the world is your oyster if you can afford it. We all have budget constraints – some more than others. But even with a tiny little training budget, you'll be able to buy at least some of what you want for your folks to grow and learn. There are many ways to buy learning. You can buy the Cadillac or the old beat up Nova, or anywhere in between. I wouldn't suggest the Nova, since that's old and likely pretty outdated. But you certainly don't have to spend millions or even hundreds of thousands to buy excellent learning for your people. Be picky, don't get sold into a full-on one stop solution, and you'll get more bang for your buck. But here's a hint: Classroom training is waaaayyyy more expensive than online. And big libraries of shorter video-based content are much more economical than hour-long courses and curriculum. With this book in your hands, you can spend less and put together your own curricula for the needs of your people. Really you can. I'm helping already, aren't I?

Here are some suggestions about how to buy learning content and resources:

First, don't be sold on the first solution you see. Don't do a quick search, find the awesome course and get so wooed by it that you just go ahead and spend on it. If the first thing you see is great (and probably expensive) I guarantee you can find something equally as good for less. Maybe you searched for leadership programs, and you came across an amazing program that was so well put together you thought, alright! That's it! Before you sign the check, dig deeper. Does that program offer everything your emerging leaders need? Does it offer most of what they need? How much will be wasted content that they won't even look at? If it truly has everything you need, they go for it. But if it doesn't, consider looking further.

Second, consider how the learning is presented. Are there multiple modalities, or is it all a talking head on the screen? If it's all just the same old talking head over and over again, chances are your learners will quickly get bored and stop watching after the first one or two videos. If the learning is more diverse they are more likely to read a little, watch a little, do an activity. Remember, too, that you need them to apply it quickly, so look for activities that are included so that they apply the learning right away. That's what makes it stick.

Third, Consider what you need versus what the program is offering. What are the topic areas you need to have covered? Are they all in there, or are there big gaps? Do you have to buy the entire program, or can you buy just the pieces you need and then find or build the rest? You can supplement a self-contained program with free content, or build some content to fill in the gaps. Before you decide to do so, though, consider how much content you'll need to supplement. Does the program offer most of the content you need, or are there huge gaps?

There is so much ready-made content out there that if you have the budget, then this is the way to go. You can find anything you need. But be smart about it. Don't use just one vendor and think you'll get everything you need. Not many elearning providers offer everything for everyone. Find several that can work with you to get you what you need.

Build

Last of all, you can build what you need. I put it last because typically it's the longest and most expensive process for getting content to your people. Sometimes it's exactly what you need to do and you know that from the start - for example, proprietary information such as how to use your custom-built internal systems. But unless you have that proprietary information to share, you're much better off starting with looking for free stuff.

But let's talk about when and how to build. As I mentioned above, there are two times when you'll want to build:

1. You have proprietary information where you just know it's not out there already, or
2. You've exhausted all other options of begging or buying.

If you have instructional designers in house, you're all set. Pass it on to them and move on to the next chapter. But if you don't, you've got a few options of how to get that custom content built.

Outsource

I'd recommend outsourcing if you have a large amount of content to build, if you don't have the time to build it, if you need it to be super-professional, or you want seriously cutting-edge technologies (like machine learning or virtual reality). There are gazillions of development houses out there who will be happy to take your money and make you some really incredible learning programs. Do your homework and find the ones that best fit your needs. I've been on both sides of the outsource relationship – as the customer who needs to hire someone, and as the contractor who is building it. So I have some experience in this arena, and here are some things I suggest that you consider when going the outsourcing route:

Decide how much you want/can do in-house: You can outsource soup to nuts, or just the main course, or just the salad… you get the idea. You can do as much in-house as possible then outsource other parts. If you have great talent that knows how to build a storyboard and has a solid understanding of instructional design, but no technical knowledge of how to put something into an online format, use them! Let them create the storyboard or outline and then have an outside company or contractor build it so it plays nice in your learning system.

Or, maybe you have some great technical expertise (some IT folks just love to play with new tools and build cool stuff) but little in-house knowledge on, say, leadership. You can have a contractor who knows leadership skills build you a storyboard and then let your IT folks have a good time building it.

Maybe you have a great graphic designer and you know everything there is to know about leadership. But your priorities are stretched like crazy. Bring on a contractor who can come in-house as a temporary employee to talk with you and get the information needed, then work with your graphic guru to come up with an idea for how to deliver it.

Hire a single ID or a group: You have many choices in who you hire to develop your learning. As I mentioned above, you can have someone come to you and be a temporary employee. This is a very popular solution, especially if you have a lot of content that you need to have created, but then the workload will drop off. If you live in a major city, I guarantee you there are tons of instructional designers for hire out there. Search on LinkedIn and you'll find many who are willing to help.

Another option is to hire a company who creates learning as their business. Again, many of these custom development houses are out there and will be happy to work with you to create your learning. Some of the advantages of using a company are that they have a diverse group of people working on your learning projects, often contributing to more creative learning programs. They also tend to move more quickly than a single designer because they have resources to which they can move work around if say, someone gets the flu. If your in-house contractor gets the flu, your timelines are shot. Disadvantages of using a company are usually financial – they will be more expensive than a single contractor.

But before you hire anyone, whether a contractor or a company, check their portfolio and ask a few questions. You'll want to know if they do all the work themselves, or if they sub-contract for things like graphics, video or voice-over. If they do, you might want to just use someone you have in-house to save some cash. Maybe they outsource the video development to an expensive video house. You don't need to pay for that if you have video capabilities in-house. What about voice-over? Do they pay for voice-over? If so, is that really necessary or can you use someone at your company who has the voice for it?

Ask about project management and timelines. How long will it take them to create the assets you need? Can they do it in the time you need it? Next week, next month, next year? Don't assume that all instructional designers will develop quickly enough for you. Some work faster than others, and some are much more detail oriented than others.

Bottom line for outsourcing is that you have lots of choices. Don't be afraid to explore like crazy and find the best option for your timeline and budget.

DIY

You can, of course, do it yourself. Even if you had no understanding of instructional design until you read this book, you can build some microlearning on your own. There are many tools out there that make it super-easy. You can write an e-book, create a talking-head video, use something like Animoto to build a short marketing-type video, use Doodly to create simple whiteboard video animations… and many, many more. Here's a little bit of my advice on the DIY route:

1. Plan ahead. Whether you're writing a short e-book or creating a video, decide before you begin creating what it is you want to say. If you are creating a video, write a script; if it's a whiteboard video, storyboard it first. For a book, make sure you have an outline. The better vision you have of what your end product will look like, the easier it will be to create. But also don't spend too much time on planning. Get most of the idea down on paper, then……
2. Use templates. Why reinvent the wheel? There are tons of templates out there for creating learning. If you don't like what's out there, alter it to meet your needs first then use it for everything you create. Many tools have templates already, but if not you can certainly find them online. This holds especially true for video. Use a format that is consistent so that your learners get used to seeing it. Maybe you use a background that is familiar to them (like an office) or images that are in-brand. Whatever you use, do it over and over and your life will be much easier when you create it.

3. Grab a SME. Subject Matter Experts can be a big help. None of us knows everything about everything! If you're going the DIY route, you're going to need someone who has the information in their head of what you want people to learn. Is it a compliance course that is proprietary to your company? Ask your compliance officer to help. Do you need people to learn about an internal process at your company? Find a manager who's been there a while who can write it all down for you. You can interview the SMEs, read documentation that they have written, or ask them to write it down for you.
4. Work with your IT team. It would be a serious bummer to build an awesome video with the most perfect learning in it, then find out your company doesn't have the bandwidth to allow thousands (or even hundreds) of users to watch it at the same time. Talk to IT about the possibilities, because if you send out an email that the video is available, you could have a LOT of people hit it at the same time. If you're offering a course, make sure the format of whatever tool you used to develop it can be played on everyone's computer. If it's an ebook, make sure the format can be read by everyone. For example, do all computers have Adobe Viewer? If not, can users install it themselves?
5. Get feedback. Ask for reviews. You'll want the SME as well as a technical expert to review it to make sure the content is correct and that it works on your technical environment.

Creating microlearning is not difficult, and there are tons of tools out there so that you don't need any technical knowledge at all. But be smart about it. Use expertise from others like IT folks and SMEs so that it's the best learning you can put out there.

Informal Learning

One type of learning we haven't talked about yet is informal learning. Informal learning is anything from a mentoring session to magazine article to a casual discussion with a co-worker over Jabber. All of these are types of informal learning. In the next chapter, we'll talk about how to manage those within the learning experience. They are typically not assets that you will beg, buy, or build, but they are assets that contribute to the learning of your people. They therefore are a part of Learning Experience Design.

7 - It's all about the experience

The learning experience is much more than just the right content to meet the needs of your learners. It's also about how they get to that content and how it works for them.

Why do we all love Netflix so much? I mean, besides the fact that they offer entertainment that we want to see. Why Netflix instead of, say, Comcast Free Movies? The main reason we love Netflix more than other movie providers is that they make it so dang easy. You log in once, and then it remembers you. It shows you the movies that are relevant to you. It remembers what you've seen before and asks you if you want to continue. It's organized in a way that makes it easy to find things you want. Really, it's a great user experience. You can also access it pretty much anywhere, anytime (unless you have an antiquated mobile plan that doesn't give you unlimited bandwidth.) This is what we mean by a great user experience.

Learning experience design is not just about getting the right learning assets that are aligned to the needs of your people. It's also ensuring that they can get to that learning, they are able to use that learning, and the experience is simple and enjoyable. If it's hard to find, takes a long time to get to, is boring or difficult to get back to if they get pulled away, they're not going to come back. Even one bad learning experience will turn off an end user forever. If, the first time they try to access a learning asset, they have to click 12 times to get to it, I guarantee they will never try again.

The experience is about the way the learning is put together, the way the learner *experiences* the learning. It's also called the Learner Journey. The learner should easily be able to access the learning asset and launch it, it should be enjoyable and not insanely boring, it should be relevant to them and to the moment they need it, and they should be able to easily get back to it, restart it, and track their progress. That seems like a lot of criteria for the experience, doesn't it? Really, its simple. Make sure it's good learning (we talked about that in the Beg, Buy or Build chapter), and make sure the end user experience is a good one. Simple, right? Since we already discussed ensuring that the content it relevant and enjoyable, we'll spend this chapter discussing the end user experience.

Accessibility

I had a client a few years ago that found that most of their employees were resistant to moving from classroom learning to elearning. When we tried to find out why, it turned out that people just really liked the classroom experience. They liked being taken away from work for a day or two and having a chance to socialize with their colleagues in an environment that was outside of the regular workday (and really, doesn't everyone?) They loved the experience of classroom learning. But of course we know they weren't learning efficiently! We know now that what they learned was mostly lost within a month. So the trick was to try to recreate what they loved about the learning experience in a more effective and efficient way of learning.

So do you know what we did? We set up elearning stations on each floor. They would get up and leave their desk if they needed to gain some knowledge during their work day. And when they went to the elearning station, guess what else they did? They socialized for a minute or two with someone else who was at the elearning station. Then they'd consume a 5 to 10 minute learning asset, go back to their desk and apply it. They continued to get the part of the experience they loved – the social aspect, away from their desk – but we were still getting more efficient and effective learning outcomes.

I'm not saying that setting up elearning stations at your company is going to give your employees a great learning experience; it probably won't, as that was a very specific example. But you do want to think about what your employees like, what is going to make them want to take the learning, and how you can ensure its enjoyable enough that they will want to do it again.

Oftentimes, people assume accessibility means Section 508. But it's not just about accommodations for people who might need some special adjustments. Accessibility includes how everyone accesses the learning assets, like at a station set away from their desk. But it also means technically, are they able to get to it? And, from where can they get to it – desktop, laptop, tablet, etc. Let's look at each of these.

Accessing the Assets

The traditional way of accessing learning assets in a corporate environment is to launch your web browser, click a link to your LMS, either search for a topic or look in your assigned learning, click the title to see the description, then click the Launch button and wait for another window to load, then watch the introduction…. Geez, we just wasted a solid 5 minutes. In that same time, we could have clicked on a link in an email that would have launched the 5-minute video and I could be mostly finished with my learning for the morning. So again, traditional ways of delivering learning? Out the window in today's fast-paced environments. There are better ways.

One, create a direct link to an asset in your learning system. This would be great for something like compliance courses, or a short video from the CEO, or even a leadership video for a targeted audience. You grab the direct link and embed it in an email message, or add it to the home page of your Intranet, or push it out through social media. A direct link eliminates the first few steps of the traditional way, because it launches the LMS, directs you right to the asset, and launches the asset. Much simpler! But direct links aren't the only way to make accessibility easy.

Two, do an end user audit of how people are accessing learning. Reduce the clicks as much as possible. The more clicks someone has to…well, click… to get to the learning, the more likely they are to give up at some point. Plus, time is limited! Let's not waste it clicking through pages of descriptions and introductions. Just get me there already, right? As an example, think about when you buy a nice new book. It's shiny and exciting – you've already read the back cover so you know you're going to like it. You peel back the front cover and see a blank dedication page. You turn to the next page and it's the title page. Then the table of contents. Then the introduction by some friend of the author. Then the author describes how to use the book. Then you have the Preface. Then, finally, Chapter 1. But Chapter 1 is so far into the book already that you got bored and ran out of time for today. So what did you read? Nothing. You got nothing from that book today. The same is true of a learning experience. Let's not waste the time of our learners. Let's get them to what they need quickly, with little fanfare, so they can learn and keep on with their day.

Therefore, it's important to regularly audit your end user experience. Here are some things to consider when doing an end user audit:
a. How are people getting to the system? Do they have to enter a URL, or is there a link from the Intranet or somewhere else? How easy is the link to find? If they can't find it, they're not going to use it.
b. From how many places do they have links to the learning system? What's the least number of clicks it takes to get them to the learning system home page? If it's more than 1, it's too many.
c. Are there direct links to learning assets on your Intranet or in static documents like Powerpoints or Word docs? Are they still working? If not, your learners will get frustrated and assume all direct

    links are "dead" links. They'll just stop using them.
d. What happens when they launch the learning system? Do they have to log in? If so, is there a way to recover a password? If I can't remember a password, I typically give up, don't you?
e. Once logged in, do they have to click a few more times to get to the learning assets that are relevant to them? Again, count clicks. How many clicks does it take?

The very best way to do an end user audit is to sit next to an end user while they access some learning that either they want or need. Watching an end user access the learning system and launch a learning asset will be very enlightening. You can walk through launching an asset yourself and answer the questions above, but you won't get the same experience. Why? Because you already know how to access learning the easiest possible way. Likely you or someone near you on your team designed the way the learning is accessed (or maybe it was a predecessor who did it really, really badly.... In which case, first fix it, then sit with an end user to audit it) and thus in your mind, it works a certain way. BUT, an end user will show you that, well, you're wrong. They will do it a way you never thought of.... So listen to them, and take a look at how they do it. Then: reduce.the.clicks.

Three, curate content based on the needs of your audience(s). I know, I know. I know what you're thinking. You're not going to read this section because we already talked about aligning content to needs and getting the right content for the right audience. Yup, we sure did. But there's even another step in making sure your end users get what they need. Curation of content. Curation is about how you get it to them, not how you align it to their needs.

HUH?? I'll explain.

You've been careful to listen to the various audiences you serve, and you've spent hours, days, weeks, carefully selecting the right content for them. Now, can they easily tell what content is aligned to what needs? Not unless you set it up for them. Do you recall how much time it took you to find the assets related to each topic? You certainly don't want your end users to have to spend that much time, or really any time at all, trying to find the assets you so carefully chose for them. So you need to curate the content - in your learning system or some other way if you're not using a learning system.

Curating means you organize the content in a way that makes sense to the end user. Group the assets, or display the assets, or assign the assets in such a way that the end user knows what assets align to what goals or competencies. So if you have, say, 15 assets related to communicating with c-level executives, group them somehow so the end user knows that these 15 courses are related to communicating with the c-suite. In some LXSs, they call these curated groups "channels". In some LMSs, they will call them "curricula". Call them whatever you want, but group things so they make sense to the end user.

Let's go back to the Netflix example. Think about how Netflix is organized. No matter how you access it, the movies and shows are organized in a way that makes sense, right? You have the "Continue Watching" row, the "Recommended for You" row, "Popular on Netflix", and then lots of other rows of movies based on things you have watched previously or types of content like TV shows or movies. Notice that some movies appear in many different rows or categories. You might see the same movie in Recommended for You that you see in Popular on Netflix. Because that movie is relevant in several ways. This is how easy your learning content should be for your end users. They should easily be able to find what they need because you have thought it through and curated it for them.

Another way to curate is to assign specific content to specific groups of people. You want the IT folks to know that you have a blockchain certification course? Assign it to them so that when they log into the LMS or LXS, they see it front and center.

Now, you don't have to have a learning system to curate content (although if you're using large amounts of content for your people it's really a "should have.") You can curate content using a simple Word document. Again, curation is about grouping content together so that users can see what it is related to. In a Word doc, create a table. On the left side column put the goal or competency or topical area that the content is meant to cover. On the right side, list the assets that are aligned to the goal or competency and link them directly to wherever that asset is sitting (web site, YouTube, TedTalk, whatever.) Voila, simple curation.

Four, provide multiple points of access. Now, if you really truly want to make it super-easy for your end users to get to the learning, then provide them with all sorts of ways to do so. Have you ever gone to Panera? A better question is, have you ever eaten Panera food? Because they give you a half dozen different ways to get their food. They make it so easy that no matter what your preference in ordering, they offer it. Order online, in an app, via phone, order in the store with a computer, order by talking to a human in the store. Have it delivered to your table, do rapid pick-up, have it delivered to your home or office….. Seriously, so many ways! You can get Panera any way you want, any time, anywhere.

Your end users should feel the same way about your learning assets. They should be able to access it wherever they want, whenever they want, in any way they want. Let them get to it in the best way for them. That means on a plane, on a train, at their desk, in their car, while doing their morning run, while doing the laundry - anytime, anywhere they want. How do we do that, you ask. I'm glad you asked.

Most LMS systems and LXS systems have a mobile component, so learning can be accessed on a phone or tablet as well as a desktop. This is obvious, right? Of course, they have a mobile app, who doesn't? It's how you set up that mobile app that's going to help your users access the learning while making dinner for their five kids. If you offer only courses that they have to watch, then they can't very well do that while driving to work, can they? But if you give them audio books, then they can listen in the car. And if you offer short videos that they can watch on their tablet while they stir the soup, well then you've given them learning anywhere anytime, right? They can read a book summary on the 15-minute subway ride, and watch a course module to follow up on that when they get to their desk.

Ensure your users have multiple ways to get to the learning, then make sure you offer the right formats so they can use that mobile app or tablet or laptop. This way, when the moment hits them to learn something, its right there. They can get to it immediately, no matter where they are.

Technical Considerations

Now, you do have to consider the technical environment you have to work with. Not all companies allow their people to get on their intranet from outside the walls. If that's you, well bummer. But you can still get great learning to your people while they are inside the walls (and even provide links to outside assets for when/if they want to access from home.) You'll need to work with your IT department for the really technical stuff. But there are some considerations you need to think about as you look at learning assets or build them, as well as when you set up a learning system. Here are a few:
1. What kind of computers do your end users have? Do they have the software necessary so they can launch the learning assets (for example, if you are offering a book summary in PDF format, do they have Adobe Reader?)
2. Do the computers have speakers? If they are going to be doing learning at their desk, do

they have headphones so they don't disturb those around them?
3. What kind of bandwidth does your company have? Is it enough that many of your people can be accessing a video at the same time? (Note: Don't assume it will work perfectly. I have worked with some very large companies that did not have enough bandwidth for even 150 people to launch a video at the same time. Really, I swear!)
4. What about mobile? If your company gives out mobile phones, are people able to load mobile apps to them? If they are using their personal phones, can they get to the learning on your network from the personal device?

These are just a few of the things to consider. There are hundreds of web sites that can help you with the questions to ask your IT department. The key is to be aware of your technical environment and ensure that the learning you are offering can be accessed and run the way you want it to. Because if users can't play it, what good is it? It's no good at all. Learning that can't be viewed isn't learning at all now, is it?

Ease of Use

I can't stress enough how important it is to make learning easy to use. If a user can easily get to an asset (because you've minimized the clicks) and launch it, and it's a really great learning asset that's relevant to them, but they can't figure out how to move around in it, you'll lose them. They're going to give up in about 10 seconds. So it's got to be easy to use. Here are some elements that make a learning asset easy (or difficult) to get through:

Navigation: Have you ever tried to watch a video online but it just sits there and doesn't move? So you look around for a play button but can't seem to find it. What do you do? Close it and give up, obviously.

People need to know how to make a thing work. Videos should play automatically when they are launched, but they should also have a pause and rewind button so users have control. If I get a phone call while a video is playing and I can't pause it, it's going to play out and I'll probably just close it up when I get back to it. Wouldn't you?

The same holds true of online courses. Users need to be able to pick where they want to go, whether they want to jump around from topic to topic, and they should be able to move forward or backward at any time. Note: There are times, such as for some compliance training topics, where a user is required to spend a certain amount of time in a course. In these cases, it's okay to have the Next button disabled for a certain amount of time on each screen. It's not fun, that's for darn sure!! But sometimes you gotta do what you gotta do.

Books, magazine articles, web pages, podcasts… any type of content you offer to your users should be easily navigable. Think about an ebook for which you can't find how to turn the page. That wouldn't be a very useful ebook, would it? I have honestly seen magazines online where I could not figure out how to get to the article I wanted to read. Some online magazines are just wayyy too complicated. Bottom line: before you offer learning that you begged or bought, make sure the navigation is easy. If you build it, be sure to build in good navigation.

Buttons: I use the word "button" but that's just a term we often hear for these types of controls. They could just be a text link or whatever. What we're talking about here is making sure that the user has the ability to exit the course easily, get back to where they left off, find help if needed, turn the sound on and off, etc. I would call these general usability controls. Again, what if the phone rings while I'm watching a video and I get sidetracked into something I have to do for my manager that's going to take the rest of the day? I'm going to close down that video - boom, right where I paused it. But tomorrow, I want to re-launch that thing and watch from where I left off.

Does it work that way? I sure hope so.

They also need to be able to make the thing work the way they want. So, maybe they don't like to listen to the video, they just want to read the transcript. Make sure they can do it that way; give them the ability to print out the transcript in a Word doc, for example.

A word about Section 508. If you don't know what that is, you can search it online. Essentially, we're talking about making sure everyone has the ability to use the learning asset; most people consider section 508 for people with disabilities, but it's really to ensure everyone has the equal ability to learn. So, someone who is hearing impaired can read a transcript, someone who is blind can listen and get the same level of knowledge as someone who has no physical impairments. Accessibility and usability mean for everyone, regardless of who they are or what they deal with in their daily life. Make sure everyone can access and use the learning assets you provide, regardless of preference or physical traits.

Tracking and Reporting

The learning experience doesn't just include the actual attendance at an event or the reading of an asset. It also includes the ability for end users to know what they took, when they took it (or read it, or attended it), if they got credit for it, and if they took an assessment, the score they got (see more on assessments below.) Part of the overall learning experience includes the ability for learners to be able to track every learning opportunity they have had. That includes if they read a magazine article, if they attended a lecture, if they met with a cohort group, as well as any online or classroom learning they registered for through your learning system. They need to be able to see what they've done.

Managers also need to be able to see what their people have done, and that is also part of the overall learning experience. Because if you are a learner who read a bunch of journal articles related to leadership, in the hopes that you will learn enough to eventually become a leader, you'd want your manager to know that, right? And managers want to know what their people are learning so that if they have a position open, or a need for a certain skill on a project, they know who has learned that skill or knowledge.

So make sure you have a way to track all types of learning. Many LMSs these days allow you to put in external learning, and certainly all LXSs allow you to track pretty much anything using xAPI. If you don't have a sophisticated learning system, use an Excel, or documentation, or file folders. But make sure that when your people learn something, you have it documented for them (and for you.)

A word about assessments and completions

Some companies and some people (like some learning leaders), put a lot of importance on assessment scores and/or completion rates of learning. They measure learning success based on how high the scores are of the assessments, or by how many people completed a learning asset or course. But in today's environment of learning experiences, is that really necessary? Not so much. If someone reads a journal article, can they learn from it? Absolutely. But is there an assessment that shows what they learned? Well of course not! What about a book? You learn new things from books all the time, right? Like this one that you are reading right now. Are you learning from it? I sure hope so! Is there an assessment? Sure, turn to Chapter 10. No, just kidding. No assessment. Iff we only track learning by assessments, we'll miss out on an awful lot of learning that our people are getting.

Also, how many people are really good at taking assessments? Well, I don't know how many but I sure know a lot of people who struggle with the formal assessments like you take in school. Those multiple choice/ essay/ short answer things that are supposed to prove that you learned something can really stress out some people. Thus, they take these assessments and do poorly. Does that mean they didn't learn? Of course not.

Tracking completions is another way some companies measure learning. But do you need to necessarily read an entire book to get something from it? Of course not. Maybe you already know the stuff I talked about in Chapters 3 and 4, so you skip that. You haven't technically completed the book, but you did learn from it. So it should be tracked on your learning record, and you shouldn't have to complete it to get credit for it.

A better way to measure what your people have learned is to understand how they apply it on the job. How will you know that the learning you have provided is effective if you're not using assessments and completions? I'll discuss that a bit more in Chapter 9.

Learning Management and Learning Experience Systems

Hopefully you have some kind of learning system that tracks the learning for you. If not, there are many options out there. In the past, it was all about learning management systems, or LMSs. If you are using an LMS, it's still good! An LMS should let you create a learning experience for your people. With an LMS, you can add content that you create, and content that you buy. It may or may not let you add content for which you have begged, like online videos or websites, or informal learning events like a cohort group.

Better yet, though, there are now learning experience platforms, or LXPs. Where an LMS is about tracking courses, an LXP is about tracking experiences. You can track anything from a YouTube video to a mentoring session to a cohort group, magazine article or a course. All of it is tracked using xAPI, so rather than managing learning, you are tracking learning experiences.

If you can't afford an LMS or LXS, no worries. Some smaller companies just don't see the need for a learning system like that. Instead, make up a system that works for you so you know what your people are doing and what they've done. If you offer classroom learning, make sure the instructor marks attendance and you somehow track it. When someone finished an online course, have them print a certificate or certify that they've done it somehow so you can track their learning for them. You can use Excel, or Word, or even a handwritten list. But just make sure you keep track of it. Trust me, you'll be glad you did.

8 – If you build it, they're not gonna come... unless you tell them about it

Just because you spend weeks or months doing your research, finding and building great learning, and ensuring the experience is top notch doesn't mean that your people are suddenly going to flock to the LMS or Intranet or wherever you serve up the learning. Two reasons they won't: either they don't know about it, or they don't know how great it is. There is no other reason why people wouldn't take the learning you are offering.

"Not true!" you say. Really? Okay what other reasons can you come up with?
-They don't feel it's relevant.
> Well, then they don't know how great it is. Because they haven't seen all the great learning that you have found that meets their needs.

-They say they don't have the time.
> Again, they don't know how great it is. Because if they did, they'd know that you're offering microlearning, which takes very little of their time, right?

-They say they can't find it easily.
> (Sigh) Clearly, they haven't tried and therefore they don't.know.how.great.it.is. Because you've put a lot of time and effort into making sure they can find it easily, right? I hope you did!

You've got to let people know that:
1. It's available,
2. It WILL meet their needs,
1. It IS easy to find,
2. They DO have the time, and
3. It IS relevant.

This is another fairly simple thing: marketing. Market, market, market and then market some more. You need to communicate like crazy, all the time, to let people know what's out there. When you change what's out there, tell them again. Remind them over and over and over (in different ways, of course) that you have created these learning experiences for them, and they are lucky to have this opportunity, and they need to get on it!

There's an old marketing adage called The Rule of 7. It says that humans need to see or hear a message at least 7 times before they take action on it. No wonder you see that dang Geiko add so many times! So make sure you are constantly marketing.

Marketing learning programs is just like marketing anything else. You want to get a message across to the audience so they buy what you're selling. Obviously, we're not asking them to pay for learning (if you are, you might want to rethink that model. Chargeback models hinder learning experiences in corporate settings. Just sayin'.) But we want them to buy into the learning. We want them to go out there and learn stuff and improve themselves and ultimately improve the company and the bottom line, right?

There are basically two types of marketing communications you want to get out there:
1. General "Don't forget about our learning programs". For example, Geiko. They have great commercials, right? How long has Geiko been putting out great commercials? A looonnnngggg time. And they are really saying the same thing as they have for the past 20 years. Geiko is good. That's a really simple message. Switch to Geiko. They haven't been touting new products or saying "Hey we're better than the other guy" all the time. They simply catch your attention and remind you

that they are here. Mike the camel, the cavemen, the gecko… simple, but effective. That's what we're talking about here. Constantly remind your audience that the learning is there for them.
2. Targeted communications on specialized programs, like a leadership program or a communications program targeted to just sales people.

Here are some ways you can communicate for both of these types of marketing:

Email "flyers"

This is the most basic form of internal corporate marketing. And honestly, it's not my favorite. Its way overused. But it can be effective in some corporate cultures, and its actually a necessary part of any marketing plan. What I mean by email "flyers" is, rather than just a basic email with text, use some images and a table to make it look like a flyer that you would get in the mail. Keep it simple, but attention grabbing. What you want is to generate some excitement so that people will want to access some learning asset that you have curated for them.

So, for example, put together an email flyer announcing that you have new customer service videos on your learning system. Remind them that customer service is a core value for the company. Tell them the videos are short (under 3 minutes), related to their work, and then provide a direct link to the videos if possible. If you can't provide a direct link, then give explicit instructions on how to easily get to the videos in your learning system (as in: search for "customer service videos" then click on the 3rd video in the list.) Also include a picture from one of the videos that's likely to spark some excitement or makes it look really cool.

Again, email flyers are not my favorite way of marketing, but they are necessary because after all, we do live in our inboxes don't we? Send them out weekly or monthly but be careful you don't do it too much. Over-marketing will mean that people just delete them as soon as they come in. They won't even look at them.

One last thought on this. If you are one of those people who can come up with witty comments a lot, or you know someone who is one of those people, then use it! If you can create a monthly email flyer that people want to open because it will make them laugh or smile, then use that! If you can give them something to look forward to weekly or monthly, and get your message across at the same time, that's the ideal marketing program right there. Use what's you've got!

Social media blasts

We're all on LinkedIn, Twitter, Instagram, etc, right? If you're not, then get an account! What are you waiting for? You need social media if you are going to reach an audience. There is no way around it. Many millennials won't read that email flyer you sent out, but they will see the post you tweeted or the image you put on Insta. Each social media platform has a specific purpose, so you really need to hit all of them. But if you have a good plan in place, it won't be all that time consuming or difficult.

Start with a plan. Decide what you are going to post on each platform. Pick a single message each week, and post that message to all the platforms your people use. For example, you want employees to learn more about communicating internally. Okay, find some assets that teach that skill. Then advertise those same assets on LinkedIn, Twitter, Facebook, Instagram, etc. And don't forget to mail it as well! The more avenues of communication you hit, the more your usage will go up.

Now, I know those are public social media forums. Twitter, for example, won't allow you to lock down who you post to. But Facebook will. You can create an internal Facebook group and post to that. You can use internal tools on your intranet to send out blasts. And you can use Twitter or Instagram, you just need to ensure you have a plan in place for ensuring nothing proprietary goes out there. You could, for example, post a link to a video on your internal learning system with a tagline like "Want to have better communication skills? Check out this video by Steven Covey." If anyone outside your organization clicks the link, it won't work for them. But those inside your firewall (assuming you've worked with IT as I suggested) should be able to launch it.

Message boards at elevators, lunchrooms, watercoolers, etc

If you have a highly dispersed company geographically, this one isn't for you. But if you have offices with lots of people in them, even if those offices are highly dispersed around the globe, message boards can work for you. We often see these at elevators. They are flat screen monitors that a company uses to get information to the employees. Basically, they're the bulletin boards of this millennium. Jump on that if your company has it! Put together a quick Powerpoint with the title of a course, a little blurb about how great it is, and how to get to it. Add a QR Code at the bottom of the screen so they can scan it with their phone and launch the asset in a mobile app. There are so many ways you can use these message boards!

Targeted programs

A targeted program works well when you have a large group that needs to learn the same set of content, or several (or more) smaller groups who need the same content. You create a program with direct links and follow up activities in a calendar invite that recurs weekly at the same time, and you set a reminder on it. Because we all live in our inboxes and Outlook calendars, don't we?

For example, the whole company needs to get better at answering the phone. You have curated a set of assets on customer service phone skills. You create a calendar invite, and in it you put a direct link to each asset, with a follow on activity after each asset (they watch a 5-minute video of how someone should answer the phone, then they write a script to share with their manager on how they will answer the phone.) You lay it out so that they watch/read one asset and complete the follow-on activity for that asset each week. And you make it a 4 to 6 week program. This works best if you have manager follow-up or cohort groups to keep everyone accountable.

Posters, tent cards, etc.

It's old school, sure. But those paper-based marketing materials can still catch the eye of your people in the cafeteria, on the bulletin board, hanging in the lobby and so on. If you mix them up with other more updated marketing, like social media blasts, it will keep learning front of mind for your target audiences. There are plenty of pre-made posters, tent cards, flyers (the traditional kind) and other paper-type marketing templates available online. You don't have to be the creative type (at least, not graphically creative) to get them out there. And they are cheap! Just the cost of paper! So if you have co-located folks and common areas, this is a great, cheap and easy way to remind people to learn.

Monthly or quarterly "what's new" updates

I've seen many companies do the newsletter monthly or quarterly. Again, this is a great way to keep learning front of mind and remind people of the types of learning they can do within your company. You can tag onto an already running company newsletter or create your own to send out (depending on what your company allows). Write a short article about the newest learning assets you've put up, or direct people to assets related to whatever the hottest topic is this month. If it's an electronic newsletter, add direct links to micro-learning pieces related to whatever you wrote about.

Contests

Everyone loves a contest, right? This works especially well with sales people, who are notoriously the most difficult to drive toward learning. Have a raffle – anyone who launches a learning asset and completes at least 3 minutes of it within a certain time frame gets their name into the raffle for, say, a new tv. Maybe a tv is too expensive for your company, so put together a few gift baskets on the cheap. Trust me, people love those things! Get creative. But make it competitive and good. How about a half day off (that's super cheap to do, and if you are HR, super simple to do as well) for anyone who completes 10 hours or more of learning within 6 months? Or a free pizza to the department that uses the most learning assets inside of a month. The key is to get people using the assets and not necessarily ensuring they learn something. So you can have a contest of "who learned the most" (maybe a Jeopardy! Type game in the cafeteria one day), but you can also have simple ones where they get something just for launching the most learning or attending the most sessions, whether or not they actually learned from them.

Video messaging

YouTube it! Or just send out videos. People love video, you know that. You love it, too, admit it! Create a quick video of some exec at your company asking people to launch a certain asset. Have someone who's good with graphics? There are free apps and software out there that allow you to create fun little cartoony or whiteboard videos to advertise. Animoto and Doodly are two that I use (I mentioned these before. I'm not promoting them, I just like them.)

Be consistent and keep it going

Don't just pick one, do it once and think everyone's going to come to the learning like magic. This takes ongoing work. You kind of have to nag, or just remind them over and over. Send an email blast at the beginning of the month. Post a social media video mid-month on the same topic. Put out posters in the office that month related to the marketing theme for the month. Send out another social media message later in the month. Send another email with links to targeted programs at the end of the month. You get the idea. This is a marketing plan, not a one-and-done thing. You've got to keep it going.

9 – Keep on keepin' on

Okay, so you've got it all done, right? You've figured out what they need, you've found or bought or built the learning assets, you've ensured the accessibility is there, and you're marketing like crazy. So DONE, right? Now really, you know I'm gonna say "NOT!" Of course you're not done! You'll NEVER be done creating learning experiences for your people. You live in an agile world, everything keeps changing. You've got to keep changing to keep up. Remember how we've been talking all this time about how things change so rapidly in the corporate environment? Yeah, that's just gonna keep changing and changing… and you're going to have to help your people keep up. With new learning experiences, constantly.

What I mean by "Keep on keepin' on" is twofold. First, you need to keep doing what you're doing. Keep talking to people around the water cooler.

Keep meeting with managers. Keep marketing the stuff that's important. Keep finding new content. But you also need to constantly evaluate how your programs are doing. Is it working? Are people actually using it? How are they using it? Let's talk data.

Data Data Everywhere

We live in a world of data. You may have noticed that after you searched for a new grill online, your Facebook feed became full of ads for grills and Home Depot outdoor furniture. Do you know why? Because data, that's why. Everything you do online is tracked somewhere. The other day, I was at home talking on the phone about my daughter staying at a Hilton in Durham North Caroline and 5 minutes later there was an ad in my Inbox from Hilton offering me a special rate on their hotel in Durham…. Obviously Alexa was listening.

So what's this got to do with learning? Well, you need to use data the same way. I don't mean stalk your learners Facebook feeds or inboxes, but you do want to know what they are doing related to learning assets. You want to know how they are using the assets you've offered, if they are using the assets you offered, and it there are other things they need that you might not have offered. And data will give you all these answers… or at least help you to see trends so you can keep giving them what they need.

There are thousands of ways to look at data. If you have someone who's really good with Excel and is nerdy like me, she might be very happy to analyze some data from your learning system (or your Excel tracking, or your Word doc, or whatever you are using.) If you don't have someone, don't fret. Here are some ideas of ways to look at the information you have about your people's learning habits:

1. Accesses. Review how many times each learner has accessed an asset in the past month, 3 months, 6 months, and year. If there are assets that have been used by lots of people and accessed many times, look at those topics to see if you need to add more resources. If there are assets that no one has looked at for 3 months or 6 months, why? Maybe you missed the target on aligning those and need to get rid of them. Or maybe the timing isn't right yet, and people will access them next month. Talk to managers to understand why people are accessing the way they are.
2. Time spent. If people are accessing an asset multiple times, are they doing it in short, 5 minute sessions? This shows they want to learn, but don't have chunks of time. Are they

accessing a single asset once for a longer time? Then they are taking more time for learning breaks. Use their patterns to drive what types of learning assets you offer in the future.
3. Access Location. If possible, if your learning system allows it, run a report of from where people accessed the learning. I don't mean home or office or subway! I mean how - a tablet or a mobile device or a PC. If people are accessing a lot from mobile devices and you've found that the time spent is short, continue offering shorter videos, podcasts, audio books and such. If you see a lot of PC accesses, consider larger assets that can be broken down into smaller chunks – like course modules or topics.

There are many many other ways to look at the data about your learners, these are just the basics. As you review what you have, you'll see trends that will help you begin to understand your learners and help you to keep on keepin' on.

One more note on data – don't keep it to yourself! Yes, you need to look at your data to see what you need to and can improve with your program, but you can also use it to gain support for the learning experiences you have created. Put your data into a few tables that make it look pretty and share it with executives. Let people know how your users are using the learning resources you are offering. The more you share, the more people will promote your learning experiences. So share away!

Keeping it Fresh

One way to completely kill your learning culture, and something I've seen happen waaayyyyy too often, is to not change up the library. Because you know, it's a lot of work to keep going out there to find those resources (or build them or buy them) and to constantly have to talk to people, and to constantly have to market new materials so people know they are there. But YOU HAVE TO! I can't stress enough how important it is to keep it fresh.

I had a client a few years back who was always looking at their data to understand how their people were using learning. Good for them, right? They were marketing, and people were accessing the learning system. But people weren't launching courses in communication skills, which is exactly what the company wanted them to do. They needed their people to get better at communicating, but they weren't taking the learning that they were told about. So, we had to figure out why. Turns out, the courses they had in their learning system about communication skills were 10 years old. Seriously, 10 years! When they bought those courses years ago, there wasn't a huge push for people to take them. So they just kind of sat there. Then someone said, "Hey, we need communication skills" and someone else said "Hey, we have courses on that" and they started pushing people to it. But the courses were so old that no one wanted to take them! Either people already saw these courses and were bored with them, or they were so outdated that the content wasn't even relevant anymore.

Bottom line: Keep it fresh. Always update your content. Even if it's still a relevant topic, find new content on that topic and replace it regularly. At a minimum, you should be refreshing your library annually if you have a decent amount of usage on it (and by that, I mean that more than half of your people have used the learning you're offering.) You need to constantly review the assets you have available and determine if you should keep them, toss them, or replace them. Use your data to drive your decisions, and then stay on top of it. If you want your people to learn and grow, you've got to keep it fresh.

And That's All Folks

So, that's all there is to it. Simple, right? Okay, so it's not a total breeze, but if you follow the guidelines I've given you here, it's not difficult to get a great learning culture going no matter what size company you are in nor what your experience and background are. Here's a quick recap:

1. The old way of learning (classroom, instructor led) is not the best way to get people to learn.
2. You need to use mircolearning so that you can have learning in the flow of work, which helps to have a culture of continuous learning, and all of that leads to learning agility.
3. Adults have specific ways that they need to learn so that they remember it and apply it.
4. Understand what is needed in your company by talking to people, understanding your mission and vision, and keeping an ear to the ground, even while grabbing your morning Starbucks.
5. There are millions of learning assets available to you in many forms. Decide what you need, then find them, buy them, or build them.
6. Curate your content so people understand its relevance and know how it applies to them.
7. The learning experience includes the right content, delivered in way that they can get to it, and is easy to navigate, track, and return to.
8. Tell your people about the learning available to them as many ways as you can. Remind them what's out there, and guide them to the resources that are most relevant to them.

9. Track what your users are doing, and look at the data regularly to see how they're using it. Then, update, update, update.

For more information and resources on everything we talked about in this little book, see Appendix A. Good luck!

Appendix A: Resources

Check out my website https://www.theagilelearningguru.com for resources that will help you with all the information I shared in this little book. You'll find marketing templates, links to more information and tools to help you build your awesome, amazing learning experiences.

www.ingramcontent.com/pod-product-compliance
Lightning Source LLC
Chambersburg PA
CBHW021832170526
45157CB00007B/2779